The Wisdom-Teachings of Nisargadatta Maharaj

A *Visual Journey*

The Wisdom-Teachings of Nisargadatta Maharaj

A Visual Journey

Edited by
Matthew Greenblatt

INNER DIRECTIONS®
The Spirit of Insight & Awakening

Inner Directions®
The Spirit of Insight & Awakening

INNER DIRECTIONS FOUNDATION
P. O. Box 130070
Carlsbad, California 92013
Tel: 800 545-9118 • 760 599-4075
www.InnerDirections.org

First edition, April 2003
Second printing, August 2007

10 9 8 7 6 5 4 3 2

Printed in Canada
Cover and interior design by Joan Greenblatt

ISBN-10: 1-878019-20-1
ISBN-13: 978-1-878019-20-2

Library of Congress Catalog Card Number: 2002116977

Don't pretend to be what
you are not, don't
refuse to be
what you
are.
—NISARGADATTA MAHARAJ

Acknowledgements

We are deeply grateful to the following people: D. K. Kshirsagar for allowing us to publish an edited version of the original dialogues he recorded; S. K. Mullarpattan, a close disciple of Nisargadatta Maharaj and his primary translator, who offered important assistance; Chittaranjan Maruti Kambli (Maharaj's son) for providing valuable details concerning Maharaj's life; and Suresh Mehta, a disciple of Maharaj, who worked closely with Inner Directions to ensure the accuracy of the translations.

The support of Anil & Chitra Deshpande, David & Uranda Stirling, and Daniel Feldman helped make this book possible.

The editorial assistance of Ronald S. Miller was invaluable, as were the comments of Prasanna Sheth, Bertram W. Salzman, Phyllis Kahaney, and Sonia Nordenson. Chetna Bhatt's creative suggestions in the overall book production were greatly appreciated.

Special thanks go to the following people who graciously shared their photographs of Maharaj with us: Dingeman Boot, Jack Kornfield, Suresh Mehta, Jozef Nauwelaerts, Gordon Paterson, Christopher Pegler, Paul Vervich, and Stephen Wolinsky.

Photo References

Page 21: The upstairs room at Khetwadi 10th Lane where Nisargadatta Maharaj met with seekers.
Page 50: Nisargadatta is seated in the second row from the bottom, immediately to the right
of the photograph.
Page 51: Siddharameshwar Maharaj, Nisargadatta's Guru.

Photo Credits

Pages 32, 40, 43, 78 © by Catherine Karnow; page 47 © Raziel Riemer; page 69 © Reuters NewMedia;
pages 71, 75, 100, 108, 110 images from Harappa.

Foreword

The teachings of Nisargadatta Maharaj as presented in this book come from a series of talks recorded between 1977 and 1979 by Dinkar Keshav Kshirsagar, a close disciple of Maharaj. In his manuscript, Kshirsagar refers to these dialogues as *nirupanas*. The word *nirupana* literally means "an investigation or examination." Maharaj informally translated the term as follows: "Insight into your true nature—what it is and how it exists—is the meaning of the word *nirupana*."

The Wisdom-Teachings of Nisargadatta Maharaj consists of edited selections from the original *nirupanas* and contains the core principles and teachings of those dialogues. The book presents a road map for inquiry into the nature of apparent individuality.

We are fortunate that Kshirsagar captured an accurate and compelling record of these dialogues of Nisargadatta Maharaj. During the two-year period in which the talks were recorded, he visited Maharaj twice a week in the small upstairs room where the sage regularly met with seekers. Kshirsagar wrote down Maharaj's poignant words as they were spoken so that he could study them at home. Maharaj glanced through these notes, approved them, and asked Kshirsagar to distribute them to fellow devotees.

Throughout these talks, Maharaj's sole intention was to bring the seeker back to the fundamental question: "What is the true nature of the 'I am' consciousness, which we experience each day upon waking?"

Originally compiled in Marathi, Maharaj's native language, the teachings were initially translated by Mrs. Damayanti Dungaji. Later, with guidance from Jean Dunn, the translation was revised by me, with a thorough review by Kshirsagar.

The atmosphere around an awakened sage has a profound quality to it. When I visited Maharaj one hot August afternoon, he was relaxing with a *bidi* in his hand and answering questions from several visitors. Although these people came from different backgrounds, Maharaj was able to read the inner nature of each one and offer the appropriate advice.

For example, to one person he said, "You have built a whole empire on the mythical idea that *you are*." To another he said, "Do not go to anyone in search of spirituality. Abide only in the Self; this will give you complete understanding. Do nothing else." When an American visitor asked him a question about grace, Maharaj replied, "Grace is always present, but not in the form of an individual. Be one with Consciousness, worship it like God or Guru, and it will be pleased with you; this is grace." Maharaj continued, "Many people are satisfied by merely feeling 'I am on the spiritual path.' One can go on endlessly in this way. Only a rare person understands what his real nature is."

Nisargadatta pointed out that realization is not an attainment, but the recognition of our innate being, grasped not intellectually but experientially. As his physical health was deteriorating in 1981, Maharaj said:

Forget me, forget my teaching. But I urge you to abide in your own Consciousness.
And only then will the understanding you need intuitively arise from within you.

Maharaj was a gifted teacher whose steadfast abidance in the Self enabled him to clearly and spontaneously provide the appropriate answer that was necessary at the moment. I am deeply fortunate to have had the opportunity to sit in his presence. May these teachings of Maharaj bring spiritual clarity and peace to all those who read them.

Suresh N. Mehta
Pleasanton, California

Introduction

A Note on the Teachings

Nisargadatta Maharaj was a sage of great simplicity, deep humility, and uncompromising principles. He did not teach a specific system or philosophy; rather, he directed people back to the truth of who and what they really are. He did this by clearly pointing out how the "I"-concept, the edifice upon which our life is built, is the fundamental cause of ignorance of our true self. As a result, we seek contentment from the objective world, forgetting that the source of all happiness is our own being.

For a realized sage such as Maharaj, there are no individuals—only the Self, or God, exists as all manifestation. Maharaj had no need to reach any goal, achieve any purpose, or possess anything at all. Yet his passion for truth and his compassion for spiritual seekers led him to skillfully free people from the psychological images and patterns of memory that give life to the separate self. He often said that we take these ideas and concepts to be reality, exchanging what is true and lasting for what is conceptual and fleeting.

Maharaj asks us to cease identifying with the mind's contents. This approach helps us transcend our sense of separateness and identify with the Self, or the Absolute. Maharaj's authority did not come from quoting scriptural passages or citing the experience of others, but from relying solely on his own immediate experience of reality. For him, it would have been hypocritical to do otherwise.

Nisargadatta says that we all know one thing for certain: that we exist. When we earnestly and steadfastly examine the nature of our waking consciousness and dwell in the sense of "I am" inherently present within it, we realize that the "objective world" is superimposed on our true nature, the Self. This direct perception leads one to the effortless and natural state of being. By continuously staying with the sense "I am," one may access that which is *prior* to it: pure Consciousness, the ultimate reality, the real "I."

Maurice Frydman, the compiler and editor of *I Am That*, writes of this approach:

> This dwelling on the sense of "I am" is the simple, easy, and Natural Yoga, the *Nisarga Yoga*. There is no secrecy in it and no dependence; no preparation is required and no initiation. Whoever is puzzled by his very existence and earnestly wants to find his own source, can grasp the ever-present sense of "I am" and dwell on it assiduously and patiently, till the clouds obscuring the mind dissolve and the heart of being is seen in all its glory.

Maharaj is the voice of our true identity, reminding us that when we identify with the mistaken sense of individuality, we also create the world with all its pain and suffering. Because the world and our physical body are simply objects in consciousness, once we cease to identify with the body as our true self, everything changes; we no longer see ourselves as separate from others.

Regarding effort, Maharaj asked people to "do their homework" if they wished to experience their true nature. He often spoke of earnestness and the need for attention. More specifically, he clarified the role of effort and effortlessness in spiritual life:

> When effort is needed, effort will appear. When effortlessness becomes essential, it will assert itself.

Jesus says that if one seeks first the Kingdom of Heaven, all things will be added to one's life. Nisargadatta Maharaj makes a similar statement in the *nirupanas*:

> The world has been created within the light of Consciousness. If you make this Consciousness a natural part of yourself, all your desires will be fulfilled.
>
> You will not come across many people who will say this so openly. I do not call myself a Yogi or a sage. Therefore, I can talk like this.

The teachings of Nisargadatta Maharaj help us awaken to the peace and happiness of our natural state. By investigating the nature of the "I," we can ultimately reach its source. Once awakened to our inherent divinity, we live timelessly and eternally in the infinite freedom of our true Self.

ABOUT THE TERMINOLOGY

Nisargadatta Maharaj uses specific words to denote the wordless reality of our true nature and an individual's awareness within this reality. He uses the word "consciousness" in two different ways: *Consciousness* (with a capital "C") denotes the Supreme Self or the Absolute. The terms *consciousness* (with a small "c"), *I amness*, *beingness*, and *knowingness*, which are often used interchangeably, indicate the sense of "I am"—the ordinary awareness that makes us conscious beings.

A BRIEF BIOGRAPHY

Nisargadatta Maharaj was born in 1897 in the coastal city of Bombay. Named Maruti Shivrampant Kambli, he was an introspective and inquisitive boy who was interested in religious and philosophical matters. When Maruti was about two years old, the family moved to its native village of Kandalgaon to look after its agricultural lands. In 1920, five years after his father's death, the twenty-three-year-old Maruti moved back to Bombay. In 1924 he married Sumatibai, and in time the couple became the parents of three children. Although Maruti began his life in the city as an office clerk, he soon started his own business, a small shop in which he sold various items, including tobacco and *bidis* (a type of handmade cigarette). The shop prospered, which enabled him to open several other businesses.

Soon after his marriage, Maruti met a teacher who introduced him to yogic practices. He carried on these practices for about two years. During this period, an intense hunger for truth stirred within him, and he enjoyed associating with people who were inclined to discuss religious and philosophical subjects. A latent desire to experience what was discussed in these talks was gradually awakening in him.

In 1932, when Maruti was thirty-five years old, one of his friends, who had been visiting a saint in Bombay, persuaded Maruti to join him on several of these visits; these proved to be the turning point in his life. The thirst for truth had ultimately led him to his guru, the respected saint, Siddharameshwar Maharaj. Maruti accepted initiation from him and began his spiritual practice with great faith and determination. Maharaj once said of the discipline he followed:

> When I met my guru, he told me: "You are not what you take yourself to be. Find out what you are. Watch the sense *I am*, find your real self." I did as he told me. All my spare time I would spend looking at myself in silence—and what a difference it made, and how soon! It took me only three years to realize my true nature.

Not long after the death of his guru, while Maruti was in a state of intense dispassion, he decided to renounce worldly life along with his prosperous businesses. He ventured out as a wandering monk, intending to spend the rest of his life in this manner. During these wanderings, which lasted about eight months, Maruti met a co-disciple of Siddharameshwar Maharaj, who persuaded him that an active life of dispassionate action was far more meaningful than such wanderings. Maruti recognized the truth of this advice and decided to return to Bombay. It was during the last leg of his journey that Maruti realized the Supreme Self.

After returning home, Maruti found that running a single shop met his modest needs. Local people soon began to recognize the glow of Self-awareness and would gather around him at the *bidi* shop. Subsequently, he took the name "Nisargadatta," which means "one who dwells in the natural state."

Later, when the light of his realization could no longer be hidden, visitors began to arrive from many parts of the world to have their spiritual doubts cleared. Over the years, more and more people visited Nisargadatta in the small mezzanine loft he had constructed at his modest Bombay residence. Maharaj saw directly into the deepest regions of their being. With a fiery intensity coupled with compassion, he skillfully guided them to the truth of their own identity.

Maharaj's spiritual lineage stems from the *Nath Sampradaya*, later known as the *Navnath Sampradaya* (lineage of nine masters), whose history goes back several centuries. The teachings of the *Nath* gurus are simple and direct. While devotional singing plays an important role, the primary emphasis is always placed on awakening to the supreme reality that shines within the heart of every being.

In 1981, Maharaj grew physically weak due to throat cancer. Yet during the last months of his life, his compassionate nature prompted him to continue meeting daily with the many spiritual seekers who traveled from all over the world to see him. Until Maharaj's body finally succumbed to the disease on September 8, 1981, the small loft at Khetwadi 10th Lane remained a focal point for many in their search for Self-Realization.

Matthew Greenblatt
Carlsbad, California

Jean Dunn, a close disciple of Maharaj and editor of several books of his talks, portrayed him this way:

"Maurice Frydman described this great teacher as 'warmhearted, tender, shrewdly humorous, absolutely fearless and true, inspiring, guiding, and supporting all who come to him.' Others have described him as a 'tiger.' He was whatever was needed: Kind, gentle, patient, abrupt, abrasive, impatient. Moods passed over him like a summer breeze, barely touching him."

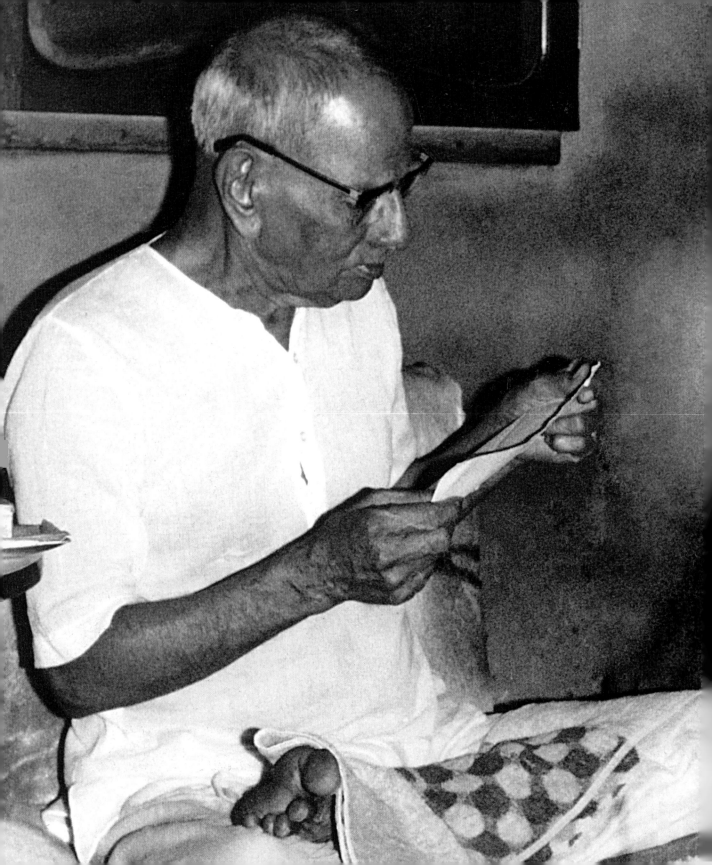

All actions happen through concepts and are managed by them.

You take for granted that you are created. This is based upon someone else's concept, which determines your happiness or unhappiness, and your ideas about birth and death.

All this is the sport of concepts in action, while you believe yourself to be the doer.

Recognize the Truth and leave aside all concepts.

One who does so goes beyond birth and death.

You become what you believe.

How powerful are the effects of beliefs! Be aware of this fact.

Know what you are
before knowing anything else.

*Have the firm conviction
that you are pure Consciousness.*

This should be done spontaneously;
it is the only way.

The mind is simply the collection
of impressions that have
been recorded since
birth.

It is occupied by thoughts,
which are based
upon its predominant concept.

Catch hold of the knower of the
mind. If you believe your
thoughts, you will be
disappointed.

Be the witness
of thoughts.

Remain as the seer.

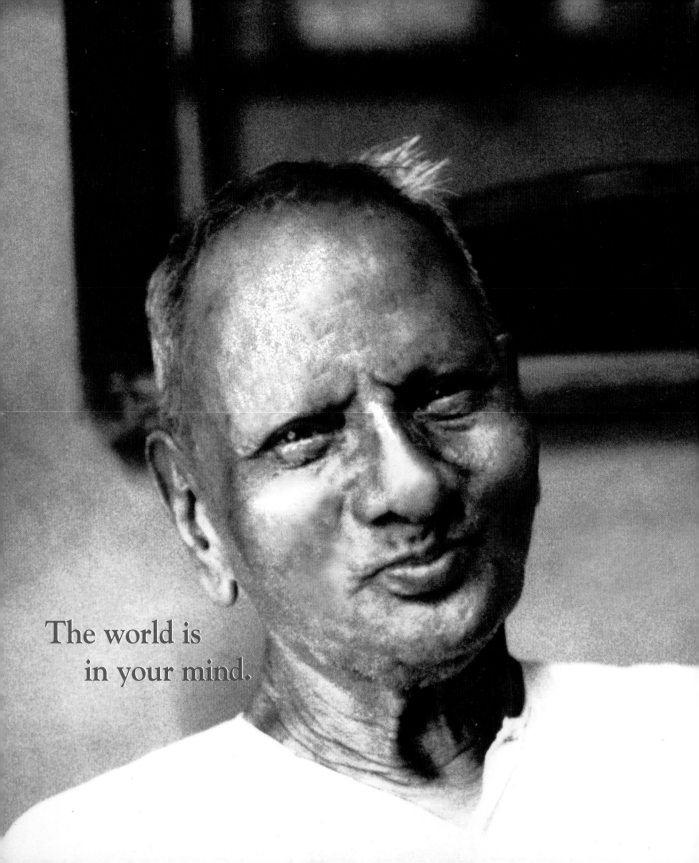

The world is
in your mind.

The mind is a concept and this concept is the mind—it gives birth to whatever it likes.
This is its nature.

When one realizes the true nature of concepts, one simultaneously realizes "That," which is without concepts.

Only the mind is born, not you.

You have put the noose of the mind around your neck.

Do not become entangled in the vacillations of your mind.

◈

When you become stabilized in your Self, the continuous commentary of the mind will stop.

Your true state is ever-existent.

The mind becomes silent as soon
as the thought-flow ceases.

You worry whether
you can function
without the
mind.

Before you were three years old,
did the mind give you
the sense of having
a form?

*The mind
has great importance
only because you have not
gone beyond it.*

When, through discrimination, you become the knower of the mind, you will understand this.

Time comes into
existence with the
sense of "I am";
then everything
takes place.

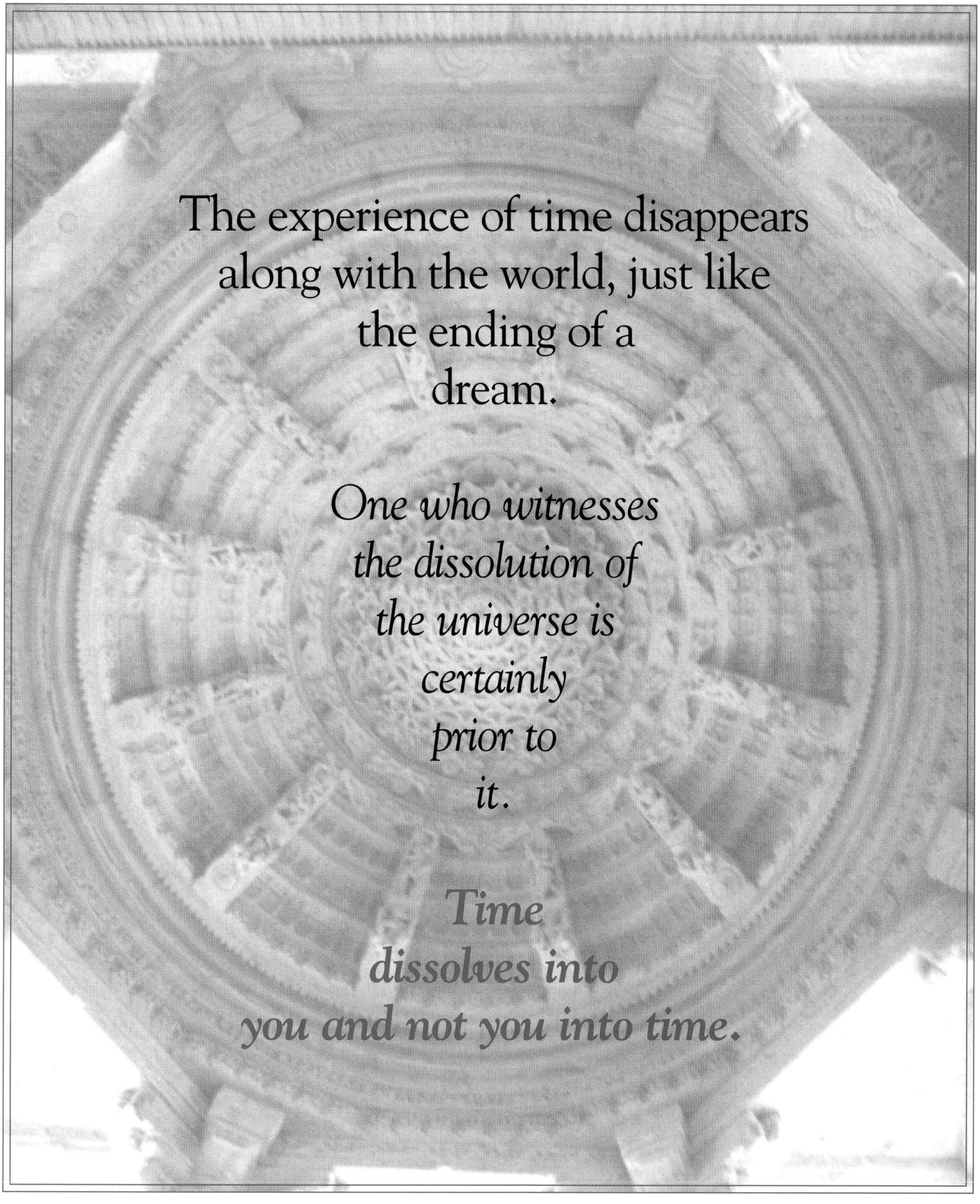

The experience of time disappears
along with the world, just like
the ending of a
dream.

One who witnesses
the dissolution of
the universe is
certainly
prior to
it.

Time
dissolves into
you and not you into time.

All names belong to time.
When you come to know
"I am," it is the birth of time.

Time shows you its own movie;
your birth is part of it.

"Who" is born?
Is it the person or is it time?

Everyday events, which are
carried out according to
the dictates of time,
have a beginning
and an end.

Only the religion of one's true nature will last to the end.

True religion is the
religion of the Self.

It lies in searching for one's true
nature and stabilizing
oneself there.

◉

Religious traditions are
based on concepts.

*There is silence when
these concepts are given up.*

People wear robes to take
advantage of a tradition.
Others fold their hands
and salute them.

Catch hold of the Consciousness
in your body so that
renunciation
has a true
meaning.

The ultimate religion
is Self-realization—it is
an unbroken and fearless
state of being.

This means to live with the
conviction that we are
pure Consciousness.

This world's existence is like the dream world of a dreamer.

We sense the world to be real, because we feel our body to be real, and vice-versa.

Why do we ask about that which has no real existence?

From the point of view of the sage, nothing has ever happened.

This is the primordial illusion:
People think
that the world
is ancient.
Actually,
it rises with your
consciousness.

When we awake from deep sleep, the feeling "I am" first arises.

This seed consciousness is the cause of experience, which in no time takes on the form of the universe.

If you see the unreality of this consciousness, the experience disappears along with the one who experiences.

The concept "I am" arose unexpectedly, and with it came the world.

Just as the dream state is untrue, the
waking state is also an appearance.
Both happen spontaneously.

Our talk is also taking place in a dream.

The individual, the world,
and the supreme Self
are all concepts.

The dealings of an entire lifetime are based upon the concept "I am."

When you try to be one with Consciousness,
the mind stands in the way.
Keep trying.
Pay attention to the source from which
the "I amness" has appeared.

Only after the concept "I am" occurs
does the idea "I am this"
or "I am that" arise.

Before this happened,
"who" was I?

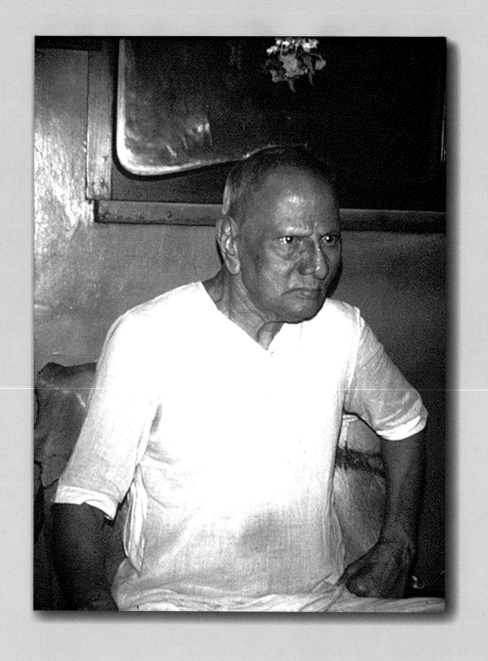

The concept "I am" veils the Absolute—
it is the source of misery and is itself untrue.

This is the essence of spirituality.

The belief
"I am"
is a memory
you take to
be yourself.

This
sensation
marks the
beginning
of time.

The nature of
this memory is
forgetfulness of
who you are.

The intellect is the play of the concept "I am."
It is the string that flies the kite.

Nondual devotion
is the devotion to our own Self.

Pay attention to "That," which is
always with you. You must feel its necessity.

Leave greatness to others.
Become so small that no one can see you.
This conviction results from growing devotion
to the supreme reality.

*You do not exist without God, and
God does not exist without you.*

श्री निसर्गदत्त महाराज

To remain without thought in the
waking state is the greatest worship.

My guru used to say:
"No matter how old you are,
you are only a child."

To hold on to the word of the guru is the
greatest service. For this purpose, you
have to give full attention to your
true nature all the time.

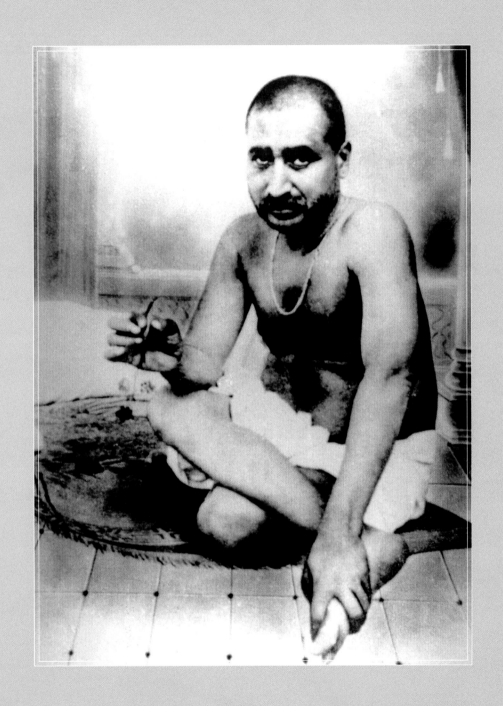

The guru is your own Self.

The foundation
of spirituality is
Self-attentiveness.

What do you wish to gain by practicing spirituality?

Realize "That," which is the root of all that is true and everlasting.

Otherwise, it is only
entertainment.

Those who teach and those
who learn all pass away.

*Whatever you take yourself to be
will come to an end.*

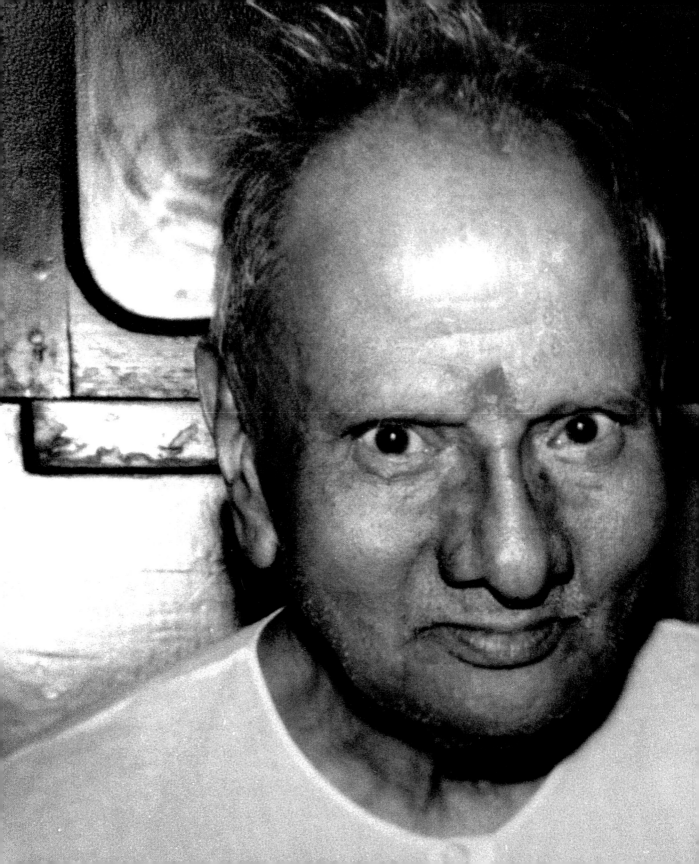

Fundamental spiritual knowledge is simple, but people unnecessarily become involved in external practices.

The essence of spirituality is to understand life properly, to find the truth and the untruth about who we are.

All that can be found is the untruth.

True spirituality is possible only when you let go of everything.

The state prior to words is nameless.

Because you take words to be true,
body-consciousness has trapped you. When you
become unattached, compassion will flow through
you, and all undesirable qualities will vanish.

Be convinced that you are separate from the senses
and that their experience is not your experience.

Pure Consciousness has never had an experience.

**It is ironic that the ego takes the body to be
itself, while trying to know its source.**

You will be free when you realize that
the pure Consciousness that is listening
now is your true nature.

*Remain as you are
in the natural state of being.*

The sense of "me" and "mine" is the natural characteristic of consciousness.

Catch hold of this quality of knowingness.

If you live life without expectations, the feeling of "mineness" will automatically fall off.

We carry on our practical life based on
what we have read and heard.

Forgetting our true nature, we act like a
king who behaves as a beggar
in his dream.

The illusion of having a shape and a form has come over you because you have forgotten your true nature.

Think of how and when this concept of beingness came about.

Your nature
is already
perfect.

Realize now that duality never existed; it is illusory.

All this was never really created, yet it is moving about.

To the awakened sage, no one lives or dies.

One without the sense of duality has no occupation, no intention or desire, and no sense of doership.

Is there really any duality?
Because you believe it, there is.
Are the sun's rays separate
from itself?

There is no creator of the world,
no sustainer, and no destroyer.
Everything happens spontaneously.

The manifestation of
consciousness is itself duality.

The root cause of duality is
that you sensed your own beingness.
The very experience of your
beingness is untrue.

The world is the creation of your own consciousness. It is seen only due to duality.
If there is no duality, there is no world.

The greatest miracle is your own beingness,
because of which this immense world
is created in an instant.
*Go to the source from
where it has arisen.*

The world will never provide an
answer to your questions.
Find out for yourself what
it is that is changeless.

The world exists within oneself.

"I am prior to everything and the knower of it."
This is the path of wisdom.

That which is seen
is the reflection
of one's own
consciousness.

*Who is prior: the world or the
one who sees the world?*

**Your waking state and
the world are not different.**

When "I amness" disappears, so does the world.
This must be seen with a very subtle
inner discrimination.

Just as what you dream is your own
and no one else can observe it,
so the world you see
is your own.

The world is a fun-game created out of one's own existence.

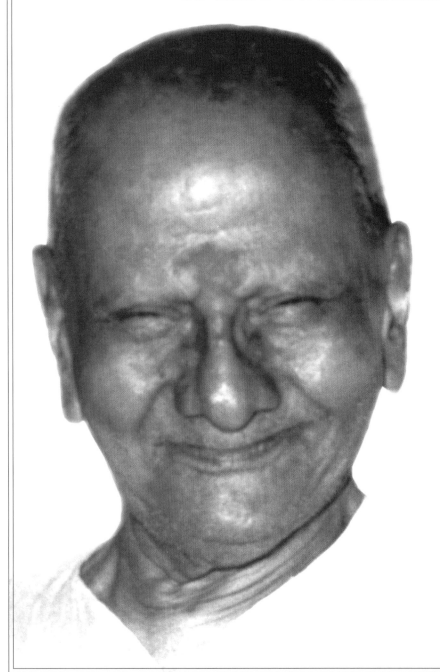

No one can stop the process of creation, sustenance, and dissolution of the world because there is no creator.

*There is nothing real
here, yet it creates
so much havoc!*

The waking state exists in
time, which is based in duality.

**You have to become your own
proof of the nondual Absolute.**
There, you will meet no other.

What we "know" becomes
the source of our
happiness or sorrow.

You were born without any existing knowledge.
*Knowingness arose only after the
birth of the body.*

Do not become stuck in what you were
taught or what you have learned.
*Eventually, you will have
to throw it all away.*

Take the opportunity
to know what you
truly are.

One who is devoted to his own Self becomes the soul of all. Who, then, will have ill will and for whom?

*One becomes helpful to others naturally,
knowing that one is not
different from them.*

*Attention should be on oneself
rather than on the affairs of others.*

Do not be enamored with wealth, fame, loved ones, etc. Hold on to your own Self.

What is known without
knowing never changes.

The greatness of the whole world lies in
the heart of the human being.

This is so simple, yet people do incredible
austerities for its sake.

In this vast Consciousness there is
no religion, no karma, and no time.
It exists prior to the sense "I am."

Do not try to know it,
but hold on to this understanding.

Truth cannot be an object of knowledge.
Only something impermanent can
be an object of knowing.

*The knower of consciousness
exists prior to it.*

Find out why and from where the experience of the
world and oneself has come about.

How were you *prior* to this experience?
This must be understood.

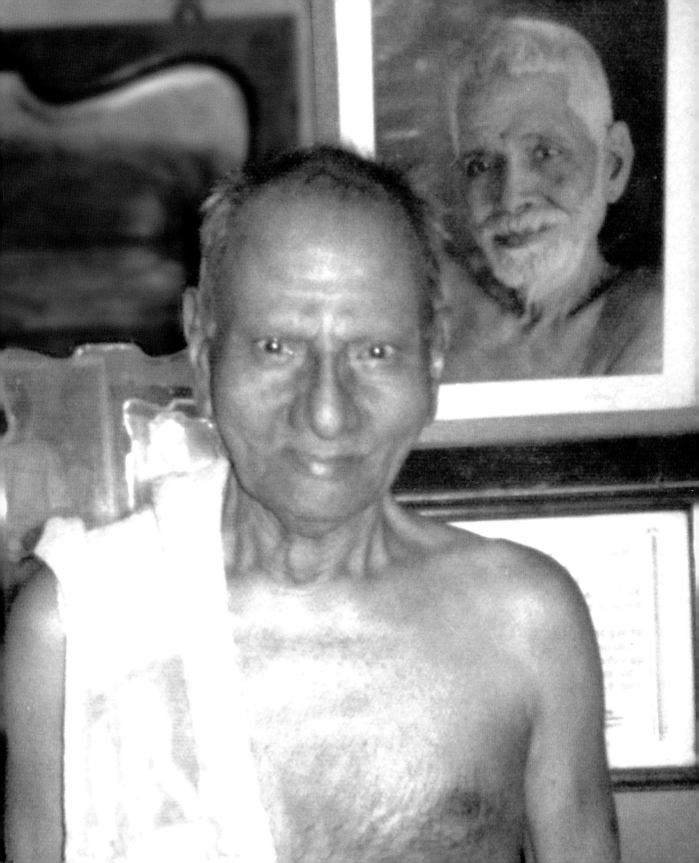

People keep busy because they
find it difficult to bear their
own consciousness.

They look for various forms of
entertainment to escape
from themselves.

*The greatest challenge lies in
looking at oneself—by
being "alone" with
oneself.*

Ignorance is simply
a failure to
realize the
Self.

Everything moves through beingness, yet its hunger is never satisfied.

Surrender without duality to Consciousness, then it will also surrender to you.

You will be like the river that becomes the sea when they merge.

This gurgling
stream of the world
is flowing out of the
love "I am."

Anger, greed, and attachment
exist but they are just
appearances.

*They are true only
for that moment, like thoughts
hanging in the sky.*

✷

Charity and love are naturally present.
They are the nature of Consciousness.
It is not you who impart them.

Do not take the trouble to acquire or renounce anything.

Desires can only be pacified through knowledge of the Self.
If you leave all desires, passions, and fears,
you will clearly see yourself.

Hope and desire are the
oils that keep the flame of life going. One whose
hopes and desires are finished has died, but is not dead.

Always remember this:
Do not become confused by attachments.
Never deviate from your own nature.

You have fragmented yourself, which is why thoughts harass you.

Do not become a slave of your own thoughts.

One who reaches the thought-free stage will not have to do anything for food or shelter. Everything will happen spontaneously without a sense of doership.

Thinking creates destiny. Concepts of yourself create your circumstances accordingly.

Consciousness witnesses everything,
but "who" witnesses
consciousness?

The feeling "I am"
is called consciousness.
Hold on to that.

There is no basis for consciousness; it has come uninvited.
It rises and then passes away.

This vast
panoramic
world is the
reflection of
your consciousness.

Though it is nameless, names give it support,
and day-to-day activities are made possible.

Birth means knowing the "I amness."
With the birth of this consciousness, the
world comes into view, along with
individual bodies, and their
joys and sorrows.

Consciousness can only observe
what undergoes change.

"That," which is eternal,
cannot be observed by
consciousness or known by it.

*Unless you meditate on this point,
the puzzle will not be solved.*

Consciousness is hard to bear, which is why people become involved in worldly activities.

You know that
no states of
being are
permanent.

Yet due to
delusion you
take them to
be true.

Spiritual seekers wander the world
with intellectual understanding,
not recognizing that the
waking state *itself*
is false.
This should be your conviction.

To give something up is not true detachment.
To know and understand that the world is
untrue is genuine detachment.

As long as you are entangled in
memory, you cannot develop further.
**Continuously hold on to what you are and
not to what you know.**

God exists wherever you are.
Remain in your own Self
and do not become
involved with
others.

God is only experiencing itself.

Consciousness is
the thief as well as the sage,
the philanthropist as well as the beggar.

One who has
realized the Truth
is not required to do
anything special for
the benefit of
the world.

*Greater than the greatest
good in life is to know
who we are.*

It is impossible to
establish order
in the world.

To
understand
the truth
that
you have
heard
requires
worthiness.

For this,
you
have to
practice
meditation.

Meditation should be on
one's own nature.
Slowly the mind will
become pure, and the
formless Consciousness
will be uncovered.

In this way, your true nature
will be understood.

You will become convinced that
whatever exists is not
separate from
yourself.

Consciousness is the
hum of beingness.

To catch hold of it is meditation.

Do not just meditate; live in meditation.
Realize you are pure *Brahman*,
the Absolute.

Be confident and persevere in this conviction.

If you want to go back to the source,
stop wandering and go on meditating.

Nothing has to be given up. Just realize
that whatever you "know" is different
from who you are.

Be firm in your determination to realize that you are formless, pure Consciousness.

The purpose of spiritual activity is
to know who you are.

Wake up and be aware
this very moment.

Spiritual effort is as easy
as it is difficult.

One who holds on to the Master's
words, "I am the self-luminous
reality," will find it easy.

To reach the supreme state, methods are of no use.

Such means are nothing but a multiplication of concepts.

However, you will continue to revel in concepts until you understand yourself.

The sense of doership is false. You are a witness, so remain like that.

This is the only practice you should perform.

You know that you exist.

Deliberate on the reason for this.

There is nothing more sacred than Self-realization. When you have this conviction, you will truly be able to live alone.

**There is no greater fortune
than Self-knowledge.**
*If it is not realized, there is
no greater misfortune.*

Compared to Self-realization, all else is
meaningless. Without faith in this truth,
you will wander about, going to various
teachers and holy places.

When Consciousness recognizes itself, it is called Self-realization.

All needs come to an end with Self-realization.
Otherwise, they will be unsatisfied even if you are the
emperor of the whole universe.

Self-realization cannot be foretold.

Some get it spontaneously; others do not get
it even with much effort. When a particular
stage is reached, there comes about an
appropriate change, and the ground
is suitably prepared.

*Then the mind, which wants to either acquire or
get rid of something, will disappear.*

This knowledge is actually easy and open;
therefore, there are not
many takers for it.

*People are attracted to what
is difficult and complicated.*

When Truth is realized, the false drops off. No special effort is required to let it go.

*The person of detachment sees
that all this is an appearance.*

With realization of the Self, it is not necessary to act in a particular manner; that would be an indication of ignorance.

To try and look impressive is a fantasy related to the body, not a characteristic of the Self.

The Self-realized person is unconcerned with how the body behaves; his conduct is not governed by any rule of law.

Self-knowledge is beyond all
words and concepts.

Though the experience of realization
can be described in many ways, the
experiencer cannot be described.

*What you have heard from other people
becomes the source of
fear, bondage, and liberation.*

Pure Knowledge is not imparted
by another; it comes unasked.
*It is the one that is listening;
it is your own true
nature.*

Love of the Self eliminates concern
with anything else; it is
without attachment.
You *are* that love
that is formless,
nameless, and
indestructible.

The source
of all love is the Self.

Your relations and possessions
will ultimately disperse.
Awaken to the Self
before this
happens.

If you try to reach the Self,
you remain separate
from it.

You *are* the Self; there is
no question of
attaining it.

Neither mind, intellect,
nor consciousness can
comprehend the Absolute.

The Self is always
the silent nondoer.

When enlightenment
dawns, you will realize
that you were never born,
nor have you
carried out any
worldly
actions.

Neither remembrance nor
forgetfulness actually exists.

*There is no awakened one;
there is only Self-realization.*

The enlightened person has no hopes, no desires, and no passions. Therefore, he has no death.

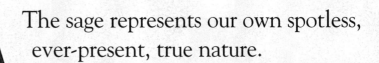

The sage represents our own spotless,
ever-present, true nature.

It is rare to find one who
really *knows*, yet does not claim
ownership of this knowledge.
"Who" is the knower?

*The realized one knows that all
this is the play of ignorance.*

The following are the last words of Maharaj before he lost his voice:
I feel the pain in the body but have no pain of
dying. I am "That" which always exists and
which is prior to manifestation.

I am not talking to a person as a "person," but to pure Consciousness.

I speak to you in the language that was yours
before words were first introduced to you.

*However, you have to understand the meaning
in the language that you have learned.*

Since space and I are not different,
wherever I go,
that will be the place
where I am already present.

I give
you the
knowledge
of my true
nature; listen
to it as if it is
your own.

About Inner Directions

Inner Directions is the imprint of the Inner Directions Foundation, a nonprofit organization dedicated to exploring self-discovery and awakening to one's essential nature.

We publish distinctive books, videos, DVDs, and audiotapes, that express the heart of authentic spirituality. Each of our titles presents an original perspective, with a clarity and insight that can only come from the experience of ultimate reality. These unique publications communicate the immediacy of *That* which is eternal and infinite within us: the nondualistic ground from which religions and spiritual traditions arise.

If you recognize the merit of an organization whose sole purpose is to disseminate works of enduring spiritual value, please consider becoming a financial supporter. To find out how you can help sponsor an upcoming publishing project, or to request a copy of the *Inner Directions Catalog*, call, write, or e-mail:

Inner Directions
P. O. Box 130070
Carlsbad, CA 92013

Tel: 760 599-4075
Fax: 760 599-4076
Orders: 800 545-9118

www.InnerDirections.org
mail@InnerDirections.org